RUBBER BAND STOCKS

A SIMPLE STRATEGY FOR TRADING STOCKS

MATTHEW R. KRATTER

WWW.TRADER.UNIVERSITY

YOUR FREE GIFT

Thanks for buying my book!

Many readers have been asking me how they can trade this strategy in a small account ($5,000 or less).

Others have asked if there is a way to use options to turbo-charge this trading strategy.

So I put together a quick bonus that answers both of these questions:

>>>**Tap Here to Get the Free Bonus**<<<

Or simply go to:

www.trader.university/rubber-band-stocks-second-edition

For my wife and children

DISCLAIMER

Neither Little Cash Machines LLC, nor any of its directors, officers, shareholders, personnel, representatives, agents, or independent contractors (collectively, the "Operator Parties") are licensed financial advisers, registered investment advisers, or registered broker-dealers. None of the Operator Parties are providing investment, financial, legal, or tax advice, and nothing in this book or at www.Trader.University (henceforth, "the Site") should be construed as such by you. This book and the Site should be used as educational tools only and are not replacements for professional investment advice.

The author and the publisher disclaim responsibility for any adverse effects resulting directly or indirectly from information contained in this book.

The full disclaimer can be found at the end of this book.

Copyright © 2018 by Little Cash Machines LLC

All rights reserved. No part of this book may be reproduced in any form without written permission from the author (matt@trader.university). Reviewers may quote brief passages in reviews.

CONTENTS

Disclaimer	vii
Your Free Gift	ix
1. The Best Way to Learn How to Trade Stocks	1
2. A Sneaky Little Trick for Finding Stocks That Are Ready to Rally	3
3. How to Tell the Fake Rubber Band Stocks from the Real Ones	10
4. Managing the Trade: Entries, Exits, Stop Losses, and Position Sizing	13
5. Real Trading Examples to Learn From	29
6. Taking the Next Step Towards a Wealthy Future	48
Also by Matthew R. Kratter	51
Your Free Gift	55
About the Author	57
Disclaimer	59

1

THE BEST WAY TO LEARN HOW TO TRADE STOCKS

What's the best way to learn how to trade stocks?

It's actually quite simple:

Pick one specific trading strategy, and focus all of your time and attention on it.

Until you have mastered it.

Too often, new traders jump from one strategy to another.

They never stay in one place long enough to learn from their mistakes.

Or to learn from their winning trades.

The trading strategy that you are about to learn is simple, and yet extremely powerful.

It's a great strategy for anyone who is just getting started trading.

In this book, I will show you how to find the right stocks to trade, and then what to do once you've found them.

A final note before we get started:

When you are first learning how to trade, it is important not to focus on the money.

You should focus on only 3 things:

- Your entry price
- Your profit target
- Your stop loss

If you can focus on just these 3 things, then the money will begin to take care of itself.

I know that this works, because that's what happened to me.

I first worked on perfecting my technique and discipline.

As these evolved, the money naturally followed.

Now it's time to turn to the details of this powerful trading strategy.

2

A SNEAKY LITTLE TRICK FOR FINDING STOCKS THAT ARE READY TO RALLY

When Warren Buffett tells us that we need to be "greedy when others are fearful," he is really just saying that we need to buy stocks when others are selling stocks.

This sounds easy in principle, but how exactly do you do it in real life?

The Rubber Band Stocks strategy is one answer to this question.

When trading this strategy, I use Bollinger Bands which look like this:

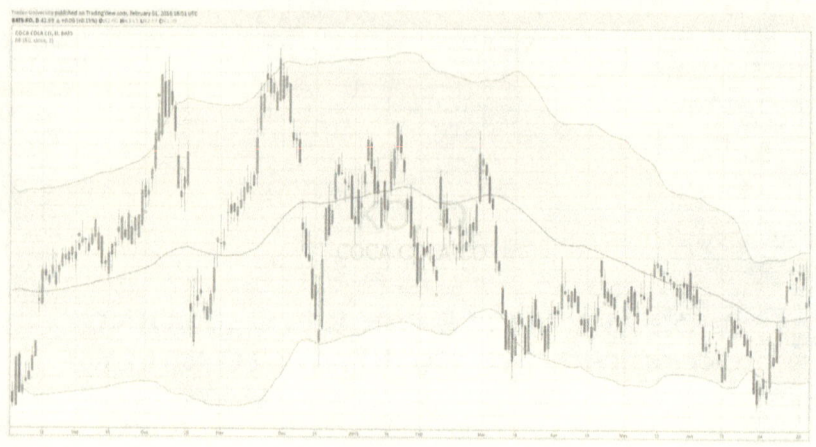

You don't need to know exactly how Bollinger Bands are calculated for now.

All you need to know is that when a stock closes below the lower Bollinger Band, it should always get your attention.

Here is a stock closing two different times below the lower Bollinger Band:

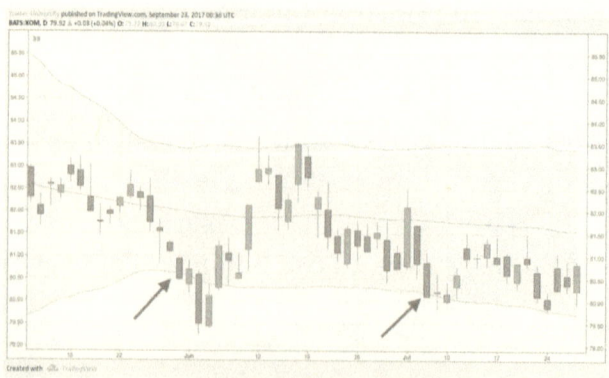

Each bar or "candlestick" represents one trading day.

If the candlestick is red, it means that the stock's closing price is lower than its opening price.

If the candlestick is green, it means that the stock's closing price is higher than its opening price.

The top of the "wick" shows the stock's daily high price, and the bottom of the "wick" shows the stock's daily low price.

I've put 2 big arrows on the chart above to show you the days on which the stock closed below the lower Bollinger Band.

The bottom of the red part of the candlestick is the closing price.

I've built a free chart that you can use with any stock here:

https://www.tradingview.com/chart/QxHMkmnE/

To use this chart, just enter a ticker in the upper right-hand box, press enter, and then double-click on the symbol to have it load on the chart.

You may need to sign up for a free account with TradingView.com in order to change the ticker in the chart.

(By the way, my only affiliation with TradingView.com is as a paying customer myself).

Here we are using daily bars, and we have set the Bollinger Bands to use an 80-period (80 days) look-back.

You will notice that the middle band is just an 80-day moving average.

The upper Bollinger Band is always two standard deviations above this moving average.

And the lower Bollinger Band is always two standard deviations below this moving average.

Under a normal distribution, approximately 95% of observations will fall between -/+ two standard deviations.

So if we close above the upper Bollinger Band, or below the lower Bollinger Band, it's definitely a fairly rare event, and we need to wake up and take notice.

Readers often ask me why I use an 80-day period, rather than another setting.

The short answer is this:

I use it simply because (after a lot of experimentation) I've found that it tends to work best in most market environments.

80 days is about 4 months of trading, since there are usually only about 20 actual trading days in every month.

There are lots of computers trading short time intervals, and lots of smart people investing over long time intervals.

It may be that the 4 month period is too long for the first group, and too short for the second group.

That leaves us to trade and profit from it.

You could certainly use a 75-day period, or 85-day period, and probably get similar results.

There is nothing magic about Bollinger Bands.

But they are especially useful for organizing data in a visual manner that our brains can quickly interpret.

As we've said, when a stock closes below the lower Bollinger Band, it should always get your attention.

A close below the lower band means one of two things:

1. The stock is ready to snap back up like a stretched rubber band; or
2. The stock is ready to trend downwards.

In order to get a stock to trade below the lower Bollinger Band, it takes an unusual amount of selling pressure.

Sometimes that selling pressure is justified, as in those cases where the stock is rapidly going to zero (think Enron or Lehman).

And sometime that selling pressure is not justified.

For example, investors may get spooked by reports of pink

slime in McDonald's hamburgers, but McDonald's apologizes, moves on, and continues to print money.

A close below the lower Bollinger Band is always a signal that we need to do further research on the stock in order to see if everyone has temporarily thrown in the towel or "capitulated."

"Capitulation" is what happens when a trader has lost so much money on a trade and is in so much mental pain, that he hits the sell button.

Fear, disgust, panic.

Those are the kinds of emotions that get a stock to trade below its lower Bollinger Band.

Then there are those sellers that are being forced to sell by their brokers, due to margin calls.

Why do we want to see capitulation in a stock?

It's simple:

Capitulation is what happens right before a stock bounces.

When the last seller has sold, the stock is extremely stretched like a rubber band.

And it is ready to snap back.

To return to the question that we began this chapter with:

"How do you buy when everyone is selling?"

The answer:

You know that everyone is selling when a stock closes below the lower Bollinger Band.

Should you always buy a stock that has just closed below the lower Bollinger Band?

Absolutely not.

We need to focus only on those stocks that have the highest probability of snapping back.

3

HOW TO TELL THE FAKE RUBBER BAND STOCKS FROM THE REAL ONES

Let's take a stock XYZ that has just had a daily close below the lower Bollinger Band, as we discussed in the last chapter.

There has obviously been a lot of selling pressure to get the stock below the lower band.

But have traders thrown in the towel or "capitulated"? If not, the stock might continue lower as they finally do throw in the towel and sell their positions.

Only stocks where traders have already thrown in the towel have the best chance of rallying.

What I'm looking for is stocks that have closed below the

lower Bollinger Band, where trader sentiment is also bearish.

In order to figure out how bearish traders are on a stock, I use StockTwits:

http://www.stocktwits.com/

Go here, type in the stock ticker, and start to get a feel for what other traders are thinking about the stock.

Traders should be saying things like:

- "She's going down."
- "This stock is acting scary. Be careful out there."
- "I'm out, live to fight another day."
- "I'm staying on the sidelines, too risky to enter here."

Do NOT buy the stock if lots of traders are saying things like:

- "Adding more here, expecting a bounce soon."
- "This is an easy double in 6 months."
- "Just one announcement about a strategic partner will send this one rocketing higher."
- "This sell-off is way overdone."
- "Starting a position. Really like it at these prices."

If a stock is trading below the lower Bollinger Band, and

the majority of traders are bearish on the stock, then you have the perfect set-up for a stock that has a high probability of snapping back.

4

MANAGING THE TRADE: ENTRIES, EXITS, STOP LOSSES, AND POSITION SIZING

Now that you have found a stock that has closed below the lower Bollinger Band and that has bearish trader sentiment surrounding it, you are ready to trade.

I usually do my research the night before, and then come up with a list of stocks to buy when the market opens in the morning.

Sometimes, I just flip through charts of the S&P 500, Nasdaq 100, Dow 30, or Russell 2000 stocks and check to see if any of them have closed below the lower Bollinger Band.

You can find these lists of stocks by just Googling something like:

"S&P 500 index component stocks"

Then I'll go to the TradingView.com chart that I gave you in Chapter 2, and just enter ticker after ticker.

Flipping through hundreds of charts every day like this can give you a good feel for the current market.

If I'm pressed for time, I will use the custom screener at StockCharts.com.

This screener currently costs $24.95/month, but is well worth the cost for the amount of time that it can potentially save you.

Again, I'm just another paying customer of StockCharts.com.

I won't make any extra money if you use them.

After you subscribe to StockCharts.com, feel free to email me at matt@trader.university if you need help setting up their custom screener to use the parameters that I specify in this book.

Back to my evening routine…

At this point, I will have generated a list of stocks that have just closed the below the lower Bollinger Band.

The next step is to check each of these stocks on StockTwits.com to see if any of them are surrounded by bearish trader sentiment.

If they are, I then add them to my final list and get ready to buy them right when the market opens the next day.

I usually try to buy them right at their previous day's closing price.

So if a stock XYZ closes below the lower Bollinger Band and closes at 40.00, I will enter a limit order at 40.00 to buy the stock the next day.

A limit order tells your broker to buy the stock, but not pay more than $40.00/share.

If the stock rallies immediately upon opening the next day, you may not get filled right away.

It often pays to be patient.

Usually the stock will trade back to the previous day's closing price at some point during the day.

If you have not been filled on your order by the end of the day, cancel your order and move on to another stock.

Or maybe try to do it again the next day with the same stock.

Sometimes I will even enter my limit orders the night before.

That way, I don't need to set my alarm, and I can sleep in, if I feel like it.

If the stock trades at or below my limit price while I'm still asleep, my trade will be executed.

If not, there's always another trade around the corner.

These days I'm using RobinHood.com to trade stocks. The best thing about this broker is that they do not charge you a commission to trade.

Before placing these limit orders, you will need to decide how much of your trading account you want to risk on each position.

When you are just getting started, never risk more than 1% of your total capital on a single trade.

You also need to know your own financial situation and comfort level.

A reminder: you should consult with your financial adviser before starting any new trading or investment strategy.

Here's how to size a position.

To make the math easy, let's say that your trading account has $10,000 in it.

Let's imagine that the stock XYZ closes at 50.00, right below the lower Bollinger Band.

After looking at the chart, you pick 45.00 as your stop loss level.

If the stock trades at 45.00, you will know that you were

wrong about the trade, and you will sell your shares immediately.

That's what a stop loss level is.

More on choosing stop loss levels in a moment.

If the stock moves from 50.00, where you will purchase it, down to 45.00, you will lose $5 per share.

If you are going to risk 1% of your trading account on this trade, that's $100 ($10,000 times 1%).

That means that you should only buy 20 shares of XYZ.

If you buy 20 shares of XYZ and it falls 5.00 (from 50 to 45), you will lose $100 (20 times 5).

So you put in a limit order to buy 20 shares of XYZ at 50.00.

Put in your limit order to buy the stock at the same price that it closed at below the lower Bollinger Band.

You can use a Day order, or a GTC ("Good 'til Cancelled") order.

A Day order will expire at the end of the trading day.

A GTC order will not expire, until you manually cancel it.

Either way, you put in your limit order to buy the stock.

You may or may not be filled on this limit order.

In order to be guaranteed a fill, the stock needs to trade at least a penny below your limit order price.

Again, if you are not filled on the first day and the stock starts to rally, you can cancel your limit order and start looking for a new stock to trade.

Or you can wait until the next day, and try again to buy the stock at your limit price (which should be the same price that the stock closed at when it first closed below the lower Bollinger Band).

As you get more experienced, you may choose to jump into a stock that is bouncing, even though you were not filled at your original limit price.

This can work well especially if the whole market is rallying.

But again this is a more advanced maneuver and judgement call.

When you are first getting started, try to trade the strategy in its purest form.

Wait to get filled at your limit price, and just move on to another stock if you are not filled.

Now let me explain how I manage a trade once it is on (i.e. once I have bought the stock).

Once I have bought the stock, I would like it to close above the middle Bollinger Band:

That's my profit target.

Again if you want to sleep in (especially if you live on the West Coast, and don't want to wake up at 6:30 am for the market open), take a look at where the middle band is the night before.

If it's at 45.00, then enter your sell limit order for 45.01, and feel free to sleep in.

Another way to take profits is to watch the stock near the market close (4 pm EST).

About 5 minutes before the market closes, take a look at where your stock is trading.

If it is trading above the middle Bollinger Band, then put in a limit order to sell the stock.

You can use the current price that the stock is trading at as your limit price.

If the stock is very liquid (as most S&P 500 stocks are), you can also probably use a market order.

This is a bit more risky for this reason:

If the stock suddenly drops, there is a chance that your market order will be filled at that new lower price.

There is also a risk with using a limit order near the market close:

If the stock moves down slightly after you enter your limit order, there is a chance that you won't get filled before the market closes.

If that happens, don't panic.

Cancel your existing limit order, and enter a new limit order (NOT market order) at the stock's closing price for the day.

Most brokers will allow you to specify that you want this order to be made available during the after-market hours, which occur after the market closes at 4 pm EST.

If this order is not filled, you can always wait until the next morning.

You can try to enter a pre-market hours sell limit order.

Or you can use a limit order right when the market opens at 9:30 am EST.

For these limit orders, you can use the closing price from the previous day.

That's the same price that stock closed at, when it closed above the middle band.

That's a good summary of how to take profits on a trade that goes your way.

Sometimes, however, a stock will continue moving lower after you purchase it.

For that reason, you should always have a stop loss level in mind when you enter a trade.

A stop loss is the level at which you will exit a trade if the stock keeps falling.

There are different ways to pick your stop loss price level.

You can pick a fixed percentage, like 2% or 5% or 10%.

If you pick a 5% stop loss, and you have entered the stock at 100, that means that you will exit the stock if it falls to 95.00.

The size of your stop loss will also depend on how much of your trading account you have put into a single stock trade.

If you only have 2% of your trading account in a trade, a loss of 10% on the trade will only be a loss of 0.20% for the trading account as a whole.

On the other hand, if you have 50% of your trading account

in a trade, a loss of 10% on the trade will be a loss of 5% for the trading account.

That's a much more serious loss to endure.

Volatile stocks (like Tesla or Netflix) will require a wider stop, like 5-10%.

Less volatile stocks (like Coke or McDonalds) can be traded with a narrower stop like 2%.

In a severe bear market, even stocks like Coke can move 5% in a single day.

And volatile stocks like Netflix can move 20% in a day.

For that reason, you will probably want to avoid using the rubber band stock strategy during volatile markets.

More on that in a later chapter.

Instead of using a percentage stop, you can also use Bollinger Bands to set your stop.

Normally, Bollinger Bands are set at +2 above the middle band and −2 standard deviations below the middle band.

But you can also add in some bands at +3 and −3 standard deviations (the blue bands below):

Or you can add in bands at +4 and −4 standard deviations (purple below):

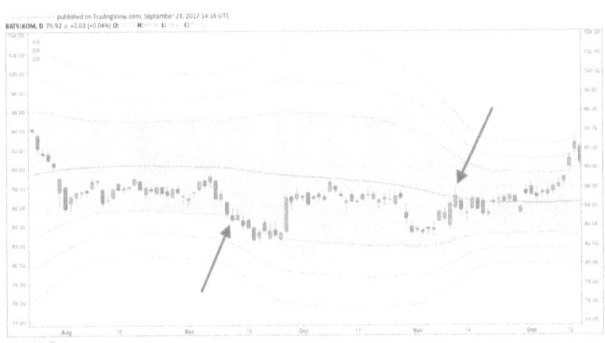

If you want to use the lower −3 Bollinger Band as your stop loss level, you will want to use the level that it is trading at on the day that you first enter the trade.

Just before you place your limit buy order, notice where the -3 Bollinger Band is trading.

You can use that price as your stop loss level when you calculate how many shares of stock to buy, as we did above.

While you are in the trade, the lower -3 Bollinger Band will continue to move around, so you'll want to write down where it was on the day that you first entered the stock.

If the stock trades below that level, you will need to honor your stop loss level and immediately exit the stock.

Some traders will take a stop loss if it looks like the stock is going to close below that level on the day.

That sometimes works.

When it doesn't, the loss that you take will be larger.

I would encourage you, when you are first getting started, to exit a stock immediately if it trades below your stop loss level.

Don't wait for the market close.

By the way, never enter your stop loss levels as a stop order with your broker.

If you do this, you risk having the market "run your stops" during the day and take you out of your position.

Keep your stop loss level on a piece of paper on your trading desk.

Don't enter the sell order until the stock is actually trading below your stop loss level.

At that point, enter a sell limit order that is right where the stock is currently trading.

You can also use a market order to get out more quickly, but you'll never know what price you are going to be filled at.

Another kind of stop loss is the "time stop."

This kind of stop can often be combined with one of the "price stops" that we have been discussing.

A "time stop" works like this:

When you buy a stock, give it 10-15 days to rally back up to the middle band.

(You can experiment with the exact number of days and see what works best in different market environments).

If the stock does not make a serious effort to at least start getting back to the middle band in a few days, that is usually a bad sign.

Exit the stock immediately at a profit or loss.

Take your capital and move on to another stock.

The advantage of a time stop is that your capital will never be tied up for too long in a stock that is going nowhere.

As we said, you can try combining a time stop loss with a price stop loss.

For example, you exit your position after 10 days (time stop loss), or the moment it loses 5% from your entry (price stop loss)-- whichever comes first.

A final note:

In a real bear market, many stocks will pierce their lower Bollinger Bands and then keep selling off for many months.

If you want to be conservative, do not trade the Rubber Band Stocks Strategy in a bear market.

If you want to be aggressive in a bear market, you can short stocks that close below their lower Bollinger Bands, rather than buying them (even if trader sentiment is bearish).

Set your stop loss at the middle band at entry, or use the middle band as a trailing stop.

If the stock closes above the middle band, you will cover (exit) your short position.

How do you know if you are in a bear market?

There are 2 easy methods that will give you an indication.

The first is this:

If you have 3 losing trades in a row using the Rubber Band Stocks Strategy, take 30 days off.

When the strategy has strings of losses, it is usually because you are currently in a bear market.

After 30 days have passed, you can try trading the strategy again (preferably trading smaller sized positions).

When the strategy is on a winning streak, you can slowly increase your position size.

When the strategy is on a losing streak, you should decrease your position size, or stop trading the strategy all together.

Great traders know how to press their bets when they are winning, and scale back their bets when they are in a losing streak.

The second method for identifying a bear market is to look at this chart and type in the symbol SPY:

https://www.tradingview.com/chart/7PeD7Qrd/

If the blue line (50-day moving average of SPY) is below the red line (200-day moving average of SPY), you are probably in a bear market.

In this case, it is probably best not to trade the strategy at all.

If the blue line is above the red line, you are probably in a bull market, and can use the Rubber Band Stock Strategy with confidence.

Remember to always trade with a clear stop loss.

All of this sounds a lot more complicated on paper than it actually is in practice.

If you want to see how this works in real life, try paper trading in a virtual stock trading account or try an experimental trade using just 1% or less of your trading account.

Don't risk a lot of money when you are just learning.

Get good at following the rules, and especially sticking to your stop losses.

5

REAL TRADING EXAMPLES TO LEARN FROM

Now let's take a look at a few real trading examples that took place in 2018.

On June 25, 2018, WDAY (the stock ticker for Workday Inc) closed below the lower 2-sigma Bollinger Band:

On this same day, trader sentiment was also quite negative, as you can see here in tweets taken from www.stocktwits.com/symbol/WDAY

- Bearish $WDAY 6/25/18. Workday will be below $100 in the next few weeks. No support. And then runs into real problems, no growth.
- Bearish $WDAY 6/25/18. Workday insiders dumping shares to muppets like crazy, at any price! Don't catch a falling knife. Protect capital.
- Bearish $WDAY 6/25/18. Still the worst large cap software stock. Billings growth of 7% in software is basically no growth. No growth and no profits= sell!

Sentiment continued to be negative through June 27, which was the day that WDAY bottomed:

- Bearish $WDAY 6/27/18. Back to February level… and it ain't over. It'll get to $110 or worst.
- Bearish $WDAY 6/27/18. Damn. Guess I'm in for the long haul. Rough day.

On June 27, 2018, WDY closed at 117.72. You could have bought it at the close, and sold it just a few days later on July 6, when it closed above the middle Bollinger Band at 128.75.

This trade produced a return of 9.37% before commissions and fees.

Here's another example:

On June 27, 2018, FDX (the stock ticker for FedEx) closed below the lower Bollinger Band:

On June 27, however, trader sentiment was still too bullish on the stock to make it a buy.

At http://www.stocktwits.com/symbol/FDX, lots of traders were saying things like:

- Bullish $FDX 6/27/18. Buying this dip.
- Bullish $FDX 6/27/18. Just awake. Up up up.
- Bullish $FDX 6/27/18. Expecting this to get back pre-earnings price in no time.
- Bullish $FDX 6/27/18. Bounce coming.

Trader sentiment turned sharply negative just the next day, June 28:

- Bearish $FDX 6/28/18. At this rate we'll be at $200 in no time.
- Bearish $FDX 6/28/18. All on plummet watch after $AMZN announces own delivery service.
- Bearish $FDX 6/28/18. Sorry longs in my opinion the downside range is between 186 and 196.
- Bearish $FDX 6/28/18. $FDX and $LMT are dead. CATASTROPHE. TRUMP WHAT HAVE YOU DONE!
- Bearish $FDX 6/28/18. I say this is a temporary stop on the train down.
- Bearish $FDX 6/28/18. I bought one stock at $250 last week now I'm panicking because the price is going down (I'm a beginner some advise wouldn't hurt).
- Bearish $FDX 6/28/18. Morgan Stanley just lowered price target.

On June 28, right as both a complete beginner and an expert analyst at Morgan Stanley were both throwing in the towel, FDX finally bottomed. The last seller had sold, stretching the stock as far down as it could go at that point.

On June 28, 2018, FDX closed at 226.67. If you bought it at the close and sold it on July 31 at 245.87 (when it first closed above the middle Bollinger Band), you made 8.47% before commissions and fees.

BAC is another interesting example of absolute panic.

On July 3, 2018, BAC (the stock ticker for Bank of America) closed below the lower Bollinger Band:

On this same day, trader sentiment was also quite negative, as you can see here in tweets taken from www.stocktwits.com/symbol/BAC

- $BAC 7/3/18. $C Hahah. Yet another rally that the financials aren't going to participate in. Every other sector making STACKS of cash. $JPM $BAC GARBAGE.
- $BAC 7/3/18. This is actually garb.
- $BAC 7/3/18. Might cut my losses, I see no positive price movement.
- $BAC 7/3/18. Excuse my language but f you bac.
- $BAC 7/3/18. Such garbage, such dumb garbage.
- $BAC 7/3/18. Embarrassing. Buffett probably scaling out on every pop at this point.
- $BAC 7/3/18. What a f'in bloodsucker.

- $BAC 7/3/18. What a pos this has gotten ridiculous.
- $BAC 7/3/18. Sold my calls at open. Thanks bye!
- Bearish $BAC 7/3/18. Waiting for earnings in this sector is like waiting for CCAR— will be a sell-off no matter what
- $BAC 7/3/18. Why is this so broken?
- Bearish $BAC 7/3/18. Will go down to 27s.
- $BAC 7/3/18. Think a pig just got slaughtered.
- $BAC 7/3/18. Where is the support??
- $BAC 7/3/18. Man this chart looks like absolute sh-t.
- $BAC 7/3/18. When will enough be enough?
- Bearish $BAC 7/3/18. What can I say? Banks should take off. I feel big money wants the little guy out first. That's US!
- $BAC 7/3/18. P-O-S.
- $BAC 7/3/18. 28 has been acting as support a number of times but it feels fake like a rug pull could F us at any moment, hope im wrong.
- Bearish $BAC 7/3/18. You're better off buying a penny stock that is not profitable.
- Bearish $BAC 7/3/18. Sell sell! Rich get richer! Under 28.00.
- $BAC 7/3/18. I can not understand this.
- $BAC 7/3/18. This is the new GE.
- $BAC 7/3/18. 13 day losing streak! All positive news and upgrades. Scam!! Someone wants to bone the little guys!

- $BAC 7/3/18. Mid 26's coming.
- Bearish $BAC 7/3/18. Will see 26's next week.
- $BAC 7/3/18. Jesus. I might have to bail on my long calls.
- Bearish $BAC 7/3/18. Tradewar vulnerable starting to drop. Vulnerable in meltdown.
- $BAC 7/3/18. Manipulation crooks criminal... guys let's boycott.
- $BAC 7/3/18. My 30 jan calls are in the trash
- $BAC 7/3/18. Calls are out in December but dam this looks bad. Almost like they are pricing in the potential for another financial crisis.
- $BAC 7/3/18. RIP calls.
- $BAC 7/3/18. This is just getting ugly.
- $BAC 7/3/18. Got a profit? TAKE IT.
- $BAC 7/3/18. Bloody day.
- $BAC 7/3/18. Lost on this trade.
- $BAC 7/3/18. WTF?
- $BAC 7/3/18. Technically severely wounded.
- $BAC 7/3/18. Until when will this sh*t continue to go down?
- $BAC 7/3/18. This is bad.
- $BAC 7/3/18. pos.
- $BAC 7/3/18. What a Sh*t Show!! Starting to hate this stock!!!
- $BAC 7/3/18. Wow this thing totally tanked today. Brutal!! I'm down 1100 on my calls. I have till next

Friday to recoup. Pray for me please.
- $BAC 7/3/18. It's broken.
- $BAC 7/3/18. Scammer.
- Bearish $BAC 7/3/18. This is when I should have shorted.
- $BAC 7/3/18. Abandon ship. Have been saying for the last two weeks on this stream that BAC is dead money. Hopefully you investors will finally agree.
- $BAC 7/3/18. 25 eoy.
- Bearish $BAC 7/3/18. Short everything.
- $BAC 7/3/18. What the hell is going on.

On July 3, 2018, when trader sentiment was at its most negative, BAC closed at 27.78. You could have bought it at the close, and sold it just a few days later on July 16, when it closed above the middle Bollinger Band at 29.78.

This trade produced a return of 7.20% before commissions and fees.

XOM is another great example from 2018.

On August 15, 2018, XOM (the stock ticker for Exxon Mobil) closed below the lower Bollinger Band:

On this same day, trader sentiment was also quite negative, as you can see here in tweets taken from www.stocktwits.com/symbol/XOM

- Bearish $XOM 8/15/18. $XOM the next GE. Sheep stock with dingleberries. 10 year H&S top.
- Bearish $XOM 8/15/18. More downside ahead.
- Bearish $XOM 8/15/18. This looks like it's headed lower.

August 15 was the very bottom for XOM's downward move. That day, the stock closed at 76.94. It then began to rally the very next day, and closed above the middle Bollinger Band on September 5, 2018 at 81.36.

This trade produced a return of 5.74% (before commissions and fees) in under 3 weeks.

Our final example is BKS (the stock ticker for Barnes & Noble), which closed below the lower Bollinger Band on September 5, 2018:

On this same day, trader sentiment was also quite negative, as you can see here in tweets taken from www.stocktwits.com/symbol/BKS

- Bearish $BKS 9/5/18. How can this survive? Bleeding cash and still paying a dividend.
- Bearish $BKS 9/5/18. This thing is gonna drop tomorrow bad.
- Bearish $BKS 9/5/18. Let's see those shorts rip n run tomorrow.
- Bearish $BKS 9/5/18. Borrowing to pay dividends? Short it down to zero. This is a good bankruptcy play, short it and buy protective calls cheap.

On the basis of this close below the lower Bollinger Band, combined with negative trader sentiment, one could certainly have bought the stock on September 5.

However, before buying a stock, you should always check to see when its next earnings report is due. For BKS, earnings were expected to be reported the very next day (September 6) before the market opened. Thus buying the stock on September 5 would have been as much of a bet on earnings as on anything else.

Earnings did come out before the market opened on September 6. The market was disappointed, as evidenced by BKS trading down as much as 8% during the day.

As a result, trader sentiment turned even more negative:

- Bearish $BKS 9/6/18. Where are these earnings for this festering megaturd?
- Bearish $BKS 9/6/18. Missed expectations by 156% lol.
- Bearish $BKS 9/6/18. If this isn't down 15-20% today, I'd be shocked. Who is buying this?
- Bearish $BKS 9/6/18. It's over, Johnny.
- Bearish $BKS 9/6/18. Obvious short, why didn't I.
- Bearish $BKS 9/6/18. It's probably too late to save it from $AMZN but each of its stores needs to operate like an independent book store.

- Bearish $BKS 9/6/18. Dropping now.
- Bearish $BKS 9/6/18. Seriously... No plan, still borrowing to pay dividends, declining sales, and it "improved" each month by not dropping as fast? Wow.
- Bearish $BKS 9/6/18. Easy money on $4 PUTS!!!
- Bearish $BKS 9/6/18. $4 9/21 PUTS only at 5 cents rn!!!! Low risk super hi reward.
- Bearish $BKS 9/6/18. Should be under $4 by.
- Bearish $BKS 9/6/18. Dumpster diving... should've held my short position smh!
- Bearish $BKS 9/6/18. Ah shoot. I should had shorted this.
- Bearish $BKS 9/6/18. Bought puts right before closing, we shall see, usually wrong so, pray for me.

You have to feel especially bad for the last commenter. This person bought puts on BKS at the absolute worst time.

This is what capitulation looks like.

It was all of this bearish sentiment and shorting of BKS that stretched the stock downwards like a rubber band.

While these traders were shorting BKS, you could have been loading up on it.

That day (September 6) BKS closed at 4.55.

The very next day, it opened up at 4.65 and proceeded to close even higher at 5.30.

As it turns out, September 6 was the very bottom for BKS's downward move. It closed above the middle Bollinger Band on September 28, 2018 at 5.80.

This trade produced a return of over 27% (before commissions and fees) in about 22 days.

Now let's look at a trade that did not work out quite so well.

On May 10, 2017, General Electric (GE) closed below the lower 2-sigma Bollinger Band at 28.70:

At the same time, trader sentiment was quite negative, so I bought the stock on the open the next day at 28.68. My limit order had been set at 28.70, but I was filled on the open at 28.68.

I then set my (mental) stop loss at the lower 3-sigma Bollinger Band at 28.38.

At first, everything was looking OK with the trade.

Then just 2 days later, the stock opened sharply lower and closed at 28.27, below my 3-sigma loss level of 28.38. I exited on the close and took a loss of 1.43% (before commissions and fees).

It's a good thing that I did.

Not only did GE not rally and close above the middle Bollinger Band, but it proceeded to sell-off even more sharply:

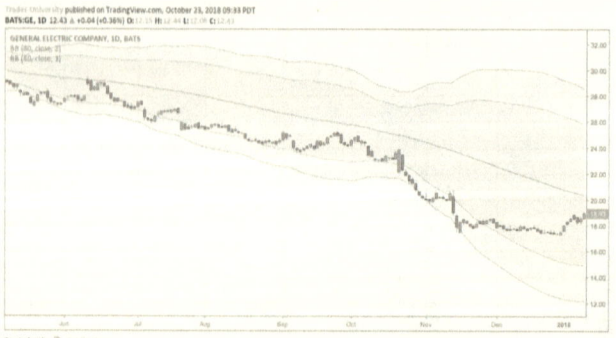

You can see my entry point at the top left-hand side of the chart. Today GE is trading at about $7/share, so the results would have been disastrous if I had continued to hold on to my position.

To become a great trader, you need to learn to always honor your stop loss levels.

You can see in the chart above that GE continued to "hug" the lower 2-sigma Bollinger Band on its way down.

This is a clear sign that the stock has transitioned from a mean-reverting regime to a down-trending regime.

Never try to step in front of a strong trend like this.

This is often called "trying to catch a falling knife," and it's how a lot of traders get badly hurt.

There is usually never a good reason to buy a stock that keeps making new 52 week lows— especially while the overall stock market keeps making new 52 week highs, as was the case when I bought GE.

Every stock that eventually goes to zero arrives there by constantly hitting new 52 week lows.

In fact, I like to make it a rule that once I get stopped out of a rubber band stock, I will not re-enter that stock for at least 1 year.

There are so many great stocks out there that there is no reason to go back to a stock that has been "abusive" to you.

I have 2 more risk management rules that will protect you.

The first risk management rule is one that we have already discussed:

If a rubber band stock does not start making its way back up to the middle band soon after you buy it, just get out.

This is a "time stop."

If my stock has not started to mean-revert in about 5-15 days, I will often get out right away.

Rubber band stocks are supposed to bounce.

If they are not bouncing right away, it's usually a good idea to get out and put your money to work in another name.

The second risk management rule is also one that we've already discussed:

Never try to trade the rubber band stock strategy in a bear market.

In a bear market, most stocks move down.

Volatility increases massively, and so the bounces become even harder to trade.

And sometimes the bounces never come.

So how do you know that you are in a bear market?

It's a complicated question.

In Chapter 4, I gave you two easy methods.

But bear markets are a complicated phenomenon.

If you want to learn more about bear markets, check out my book here:

Bear Market Trading Strategies

or here:

www.trader-books.com

To review:

Never trade the Rubber Band Stocks Strategy when the SPY (the S&P 500) 50-day moving average is trading below its 200-day moving average.

This is how that looked during the 2008-2009 bear market:

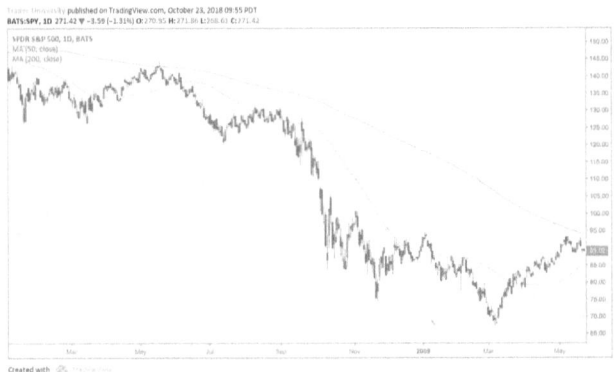

When the 50-day moving average for the SPY crosses below the 200-day moving average (what is often called a "death cross"), it can be a sign that a new bear market is beginning.

Especially if you have had a strong bull market for the past 7 or more years.

The best form of risk management in trading is often summed up by this formula:

Do more of what's working, and less of what's not working

If you have a few losing trades in a row with rubber band stocks, it's a good sign that the current market is not friendly to this particular strategy.

If the SPY 50-day moving average is below the SPY 200-day moving average, you will often do better by shorting stocks into their rallies, rather than by trying to buy their dips.

So be flexible, and learn to adapt to current market conditions.

An experienced trader knows that he can only take what the market gives him.

Always trade with stop losses, and never let a losing trade turn into a "long-term holding."

Even if it's a blue chip name like Ford or General Electric.

Yesterday's blue chip stock is tomorrow's bankruptcy.

Learn to listen to a stock's price action, and you will do much better than reading any financial news.

It also really helps to be able to read and analyze a company's financial statements.

I hope to be able to teach you how to do this in a later book.

As traders, we want to be able to use every tool at our disposal, whether it is technical analysis, indicators, or fundamental analysis.

At Trader University, I teach traders and investors all of these subjects.

6
TAKING THE NEXT STEP TOWARDS A WEALTHY FUTURE

You are now ready to trade the Rubber Band Stocks Strategy for yourself.

All you need to do is to find stocks that meet the following requirements:

1. The stock has just closed below the lower Bollinger Band.
2. There is extremely bearish trader sentiment surrounding your stock.

That's it!

The best way to learn about trading is to just start doing it.

Start with very small positions, and then slowly increase them as your capital (and your confidence!) increases.

There's no better way to learn than simply by doing.

Also before you start, make sure that you know how to size your trade, and how to manage your trade using a profit target and a stop loss, as we discussed in this book.

If you do not have a lot of trading experience, I suggest that you first practice trading the Rubber Band Stocks Strategy without using real money.

Any number of brokers will let you open up a practice (paper-trading) account.

I have not tried them myself, but my students have reported good things about the paper trading accounts available here:

https://www.thinkorswim.com/t/index.html#!/pmregister

Whenever I read a new book like this, I try to figure out some concrete steps that I can immediately take to put into action the lessons that I've learned.

Now it's time for you to take action too.

Don't just put this book down and do nothing.

Open up a brokerage account at Robinhood.com with a

small amount of money and start trading the Rubber Band Stocks Strategy.

The best way to learn how to trade is...

To start trading.

Keep your positions small at first, while you are learning.

As you gain more experience, you will begin to know when to bet big, and when to keep your bets small.

Thanks for purchasing this book and reading it all the way to the end.

If you enjoyed this book and found it useful, I'd be very grateful if you'd post an honest review on Amazon.

All that you need to do is to **click here** (or go to www.trader-books.com) and then click on the correct book cover.

Then click the blue link next to the yellow stars that says "customer reviews."

You'll then see a gray button that says "Write a customer review"—click that and you're good to go.

Also, if you would like to learn more ways to make money, check out my other books on the next page.

ALSO BY MATTHEW R. KRATTER

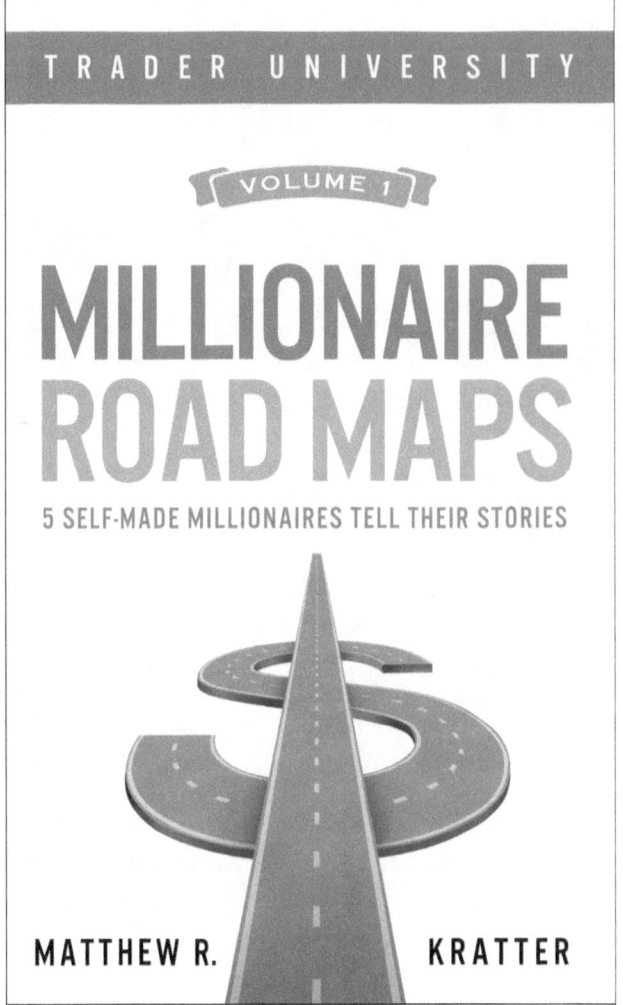

Click here to buy this book on Amazon

Or simply go to www.trader.university and click on the

"Books" tab.

TRADER UNIVERSITY

THE LITTLE BLACK BOOK OF STOCK MARKET SECRETS

MATTHEW R. KRATTER

Click here to buy this book on Amazon

Or simply go to www.trader.university and click on the

"Books" tab.

YOUR FREE GIFT

Thanks for buying my book!

Many readers have been asking me how they can trade this strategy in a small account ($5,000 or less).

Others have asked if there is a way to use options to turbo-charge this trading strategy.

So I put together a quick bonus that answers both of these questions:

>>>Tap Here to Get the Free Bonus<<<

Or simply go to:

www.trader.university/rubber-band-stocks-second-edition

ABOUT THE AUTHOR

Hi there!

My name is Matthew Kratter.

I am the founder of Trader University, and the best-selling author of multiple books on trading and investing.

I have more than 20 years of trading experience, including working at multiple hedge funds.

Most individual traders and investors are at a huge disadvantage when it comes to the markets.

Most are unable to invest in hedge funds.

Yet, when they trade their own money, they are competing against computer algorithms, math PhD's, and multi-billion dollar hedge funds.

I've been on the inside of many hedge funds.

I know how professional traders and investors think and approach the markets.

And I am committed to sharing their trading strategies with you in my books and courses.

When I am not trading or writing new books, I enjoy skiing, hiking, and otherwise hanging out in the Rocky Mountains with my wife, kids, and dogs.

If you enjoyed this book, you may also enjoy my other books and courses, which are available here:

http://www.trader.university

To see the books, just click on the tab that says "Audible" for my audio books, or on the tab "Kindle/Paperback."

Or send me an email at matt@trader.university.

I would love to hear from you.

DISCLAIMER

While the author has used his best efforts in preparing this book, he makes no representations or warranties with respect to the accuracy or completeness of the contents of this book and specifically disclaims any implied warranties or merchantability or fitness for a particular purpose. The advice and strategies contained herein may not be suitable for your situation.

You should consult with a legal, financial, tax, health or other professional where appropriate. Neither the publisher nor the author shall be liable for any loss of profit or any other commercial damages, including but not limited to special, incidental, consequential, or other damages.

This book is for educational purposes only. The views

expressed are those of the author alone, and should not be taken as expert instruction or commands. The reader is responsible for his or her own actions.

Adherence to all applicable laws and regulations, including international, federal, state, and local laws, is the sole responsibility of the purchaser or reader.

Neither the author nor the publisher assumes any responsibility or liability whatsoever on the behalf of the purchaser or reader of these materials.

Any perceived slight of any individual or organization is purely unintentional.

Past performance is not necessarily indicative of future performance.

Forex, futures, stock, and options trading is not appropriate for everyone.

There is a substantial risk of loss associated with trading these markets. Losses can and will occur.

No system or methodology has ever been developed that can guarantee profits or ensure freedom from losses. Nor will it likely ever be.

No representation or implication is being made that using the methodologies or systems or the information

contained within this book will generate profits or ensure freedom from losses.

The information contained in this book is for educational purposes only and should NOT be taken as investment advice. Examples presented here are not solicitations to buy or sell. The author, publisher, and all affiliates assume no responsibility for your trading results.

There is a high risk in trading.

HYPOTHETICAL OR SIMULATED PERFORMANCE RESULTS HAVE CERTAIN LIMITATIONS.

UNLIKE AN ACTUAL PERFORMANCE RECORD, SIMULATED RESULTS DO NOT REPRESENT ACTUAL TRADING. ALSO, SINCE THE TRADES HAVE NOT BEEN EXECUTED, THE RESULTS MAY HAVE UNDER-OR-OVER COMPENSATED FOR THE IMPACT, IF ANY, OF CERTAIN MARKET FACTORS, SUCH AS THE LACK OF LIQUIDITY.

SIMULATED TRADING PROGRAMS IN GENERAL ARE ALSO SUBJECT TO THE FACT THAT THEY ARE DESIGNED WITH THE BENEFIT OF HINDSIGHT. NO REPRESENTATION IS BEING MADE THAT ANY ACCOUNT WILL OR IS LIKELY TO ACHIEVE PROFIT OR LOSSES SIMILAR TO THOSE SHOWN.

www.ingramcontent.com/pod-product-compliance
Lightning Source LLC
Chambersburg PA
CBHW021506210526
45463CB00002B/917